T0095225

BULLYING MUST GO

SAYS A NORFOLK 17 HERO

Dr. Delores Johnson Brown

BULLYING MUST GO
SAYS A NORFOLK 17 HERO

iUniverse books may be ordered through booksellers or by contacting:

iUniverse
1663 Liberty Drive
Bloomington, IN 47403
www.iuniverse.com
1-800-Authors (1-800-288-4677)

Because of the dynamic nature of the Internet, any web addresses or links contained in this book may have changed since publication and may no longer be valid. The views expressed in this work are solely those of the author and do not necessarily reflect the views of the publisher, and the publisher hereby disclaims any responsibility for them.

Any people depicted in stock imagery provided by Thinkstock are models, and such images are being used for illustrative purposes only. Certain stock imagery © Thinkstock.

ISBN: 978-1-4917-7861-6 (sc)
ISBN: 978-1-4917-7862-3 (e)

Library of Congress Control Number: 2015915941

Print information available on the last page.

iUniverse rev. date: 09/24/2015

Table of Contents

Chapter 1 Let's Get Acquainted 1

Chapter 2 Rough Times at Norview High 10

Chapter 3 The Fight for Integration 13

Chapter 4 High School & Universities 18

Chapter 5 Resolutions, Awards & Certificates 20

Chapter 6 Meet all Of The Norfolk 17 23

Chapter 7 Closing, From the Heart 24

Chapter 8 Happy Birthday to Me 25

About the Author 43

Table of Contents

Chapter 1 1
Chapter 2 3
Chapter 3 5
Chapter 4 9
Chapter 5 20
Chapter 6 26
Chapter 7 34
Chapter 8 ....
About the Author ....

Chapter 1

Let's Get Acquainted

Dear Family and Friends

Even though some of you are meeting me for the first time, I already consider you my friend, not just an acquaintance. Nobody is a stranger to me and it won't be long before you'll be convinced that we really are friends. My name is Dr. Delores Johnson Brown. I was born Delores Johnson on March 20, 1942 at City Hospital in Baltimore, MD.

I retired from Norfolk Public Schools in 1996, after completing twenty-eight years. I was a Reading Specialist and an educational specialist.

My mother was Mrs. Sarah Catherine Goodman Johnson born on May 16, 1915 in Clinton, NC. She passed on January 1, 1981. She resided in Portsmouth, Virginia. She retired from the Norfolk Virginia Air Station. My father was Mr. Albert Harold Johnson born on January 28, 1914 in Clinton, NC. He passed on April 15, 1949. He served in the U. S. Navy and was stationed in Norfolk, VA. There were six children in my family. My brother, Lyndell Johnson was the oldest, born on October 8, 1931 in Clinton, N.C. He expired on May 16, 2009, on my mother's birthday. He retired from the U. S. Army and the U. S. Postal Service. Next, was Mrs. Frances Adelaide Johnson Holland who was the oldest girl and was born on July 9, 1935 in Wilmington, N.C. She expired on March 10, 1985. She retired from the Bendix Corporation as an electrical engineer. She resided in Newark, NJ. My second brother, James Lewis Johnson, nick named Jit. He was born on April 4, 1938 in Wilmington, N.C. He expired in 1963. He resided in

Boca Raton, FL. He served in the U. S. Air Force. My third brother was Carl Harold Johnson, born on January 29, 1940 in Baltimore, MD. He expired on November 5, 1981, the same year that I lost my mother, in Portsmouth, VA. He served in the U. S. Air Force too. My baby sister is Sharon Baker, born on November 7, 1954. She resides in Portsmouth, VA. and is a residential engineer. Well, you've met my first family let's move on to my second or immediate family.

I am married to Mr. Allen B. Brown Sr. who was born on December 8, 1937 in Norfolk, VA. He retired from the United States Postal Service as a Manager of Distribution Operations. We had three sons and they all were born in Norfolk, VA. The first one is Allen B. Brown Jr. who was born on January 14, 1960. He lives in the same neighborhood as we do now, on Plantation Lakes Circle in Chesapeake, VA. Our second son was Alvalon Brown who was born on August 7, 1961 and he expired on December 14, 2010. Our baby boy is Altonio Lyndell Brown who was born on June 26, 1969. He lives in Norfolk, VA. He isn't very far away from our neighborhood. All of our sons attended Norfolk State University and went on to become International Longshoremen and checkers for the Shortshoremen Association.

Now, meet our grandchildren: Little Allen, Altiya, Marcia, Starr and Little Tony. Well, now that you've met us, I've got to tell you more that's relative to me, personally. After all, this is my autobiography, all about me.

Oh, I forgot to tell you that I'm one of The Norfolk 17 and I'll explain that later. Even though Edward R. Morrow, a national well known news reporter (CBS TV) and his crew, came to Norfolk and made a documentary on the Norfolk 17 back in 1958, our struggle was not publicized as much as down in the deeper south, like Mississippi Alabama and other southern states. The largest Naval Base in the world is here in Norfolk, Virginia. That might have had something to do with our low profile, I really don't know.

Several years ago, Barbara Sierra, a local news reporter (CBS TV) focused us on TV for a full hour. That program was broadcast locally for Black History Month over several years. She won an award for that historical documentary. It was very well done. We were interviewed and enjoyed it very much.

Recently, the Ed Show (MSNBC) featured The Norfolk 17and gave a stipend for a very brief segment of his program. He did not forget his hometown. We were recognized nationally!

More is to come, you just wait. We must get back to me. My nickname is "Pumpkin" and nobody else calls me that but another one of The Norfolk 17, Patricia Godbolt White. I even told her that my godmother, Miss Flossie named me that because I was so chubby and round plus my complexion reminded her of a pumpkin. Sometimes, I wish I had never told Pat that. Actually, I like it very much, when she calls me "Pumpkin" it reminds me that we go way back and I just love that. We went to Oakwood Elementary School, Ruffner Jr. High (Ruffner Academy), Booker T. Washington High, (BTW) and Norview High (NH) together. We were in the Girl Scouts and the Spelling Bee together too. Oh, we sang in the Oakwood Elementary School Chorus together. We were close friends and shared secrets with each other. We are both members of Delta Sigma Theta Sorority, Inc. She and Johnnie Rouse, (now decease) another Norfolk 17 were my mentors when I was preparing to become a Delta. Pat and I lived in the same neighborhoods, Chesapeake Gardens as children and Poplar Halls, as adults. Pumpkin was not my only nickname. It was my Portsmouth, VA nickname while I lived with Miss Flossie.

She was good as gold, but she tore me up with a switch, whenever I didn't follow rules or especially if I didn't dusk perfectly. Pumpkin hates to dusk even today. Don't rub your hands on my furniture, wearing white gloves! I might be terribly embarrassed. You just might remind me of those whippings! Maybe they made me a better person, I sure hope so. Remember, spare the rod and spoil the child. She sure didn't spoil me when it came down to dusting.

My other nickname is "Tootsie." Now, don't ask me why my daddy loved to call me that. He knew it made me feel really loved and who does not want to feel loved? Whenever, he'd ask me, "Tootsie, how much do you love me?" I'd spread out my arms as wide as I possibly could and say, "Daddy, I love you very, very much!" Then he'd say, "Well, go in the room and bring me my slippers."

Before he could say half of that sentence, I'd say, "Oh Daddy, I only loved you only this much, Daddy." I would hold up my two pointer fingers almost touching. Then, I'd say, "Daddy, I changed my mind, I only love you just a little bit." Then he'd say, "Where's my belt?" I'd take off and fly into the bedroom and get his slippers and jump back up in his lap. We'd play finger games, nursery rhymes and he would read stories to me. He was a teacher in the Navy and I decided then that I was going to be a teacher too. You see, nobody had time to play with me but my Dad and I guess that's why I like to go way back to the good ole days. Wait until I tell you what happened to me when I was only two years old. That's enough about my nicknames! We'll get there sooner or later.

Yes, let's go way back to when I was only two years old and the U.S. Navy transferred my family from Baltimore to Norfolk. One day I was looking out of our second floor window and I saw a bird flying around. I told my brother Carl, that I could fly like that bird and before he could look, I jumped out of the window, landed on a chicken and ended up in the hospital. I wonder did that chicken save my life? Anyway, when it was time for me to be discharged from the hospital, I was having such a good time that I didn't want to leave. Maybe I didn't want to return to that dresser drawer that was my crib. I really loved all the attention I was receiving and eating all that good food. Yes, times were hard during that time. I didn't know that. I was just having a good time, even in the hospital.

Even though, my dad was a teacher in the navy and my mom was a domestic worker at that time, we didn't have very much money to live on because my dad had a drinking problem. When he got paid, he headed straight to the package store, that's what we call the ABC Store where they sell alcohol. After over indulging himself, he wouldn't wake up and return to duty like he was supposed to do. Therefore, he'd end up in the brig, we know it as the jail. We visited him quite often while he was in the brig.

I really missed him when he was in the brig. I enjoyed visiting him in the brig because I got to meet a lot of people. I really love people, even at this current time, I really love all people.

One day while we were visiting my dad in the brig, I saw a lady getting ready to scrape the mustard and onions off her hot dog into the trashcan. I ran over to that lady and asked her if I could have them because I was so hungry. That lady was Miss Flossie, she bought me a hot dog and I gave her a great big hug. She asked me if I would like to go home with her and I said," yes mam." She told my parents that they wouldn't have to pay her anything because she didn't have any children and she would take very good care of me. I lived with her from age two until I was ten. She provided me with lots of food, clothing, toys, dance lessons, Girl Scouts, and birthday parties etc. She even hired a photographer to take pictures at my parties. She paid the sailors, who rented rooms from her, to bring dolls from all over the world back to me. She really spoiled me in a good way as long as I cleaned up the house perfectly. Whenever I didn't dust to her perfection, I'd get a whipping. Now, I'm sure I deserved some of those whippings and perhaps they attributed to my becoming a better person, like I said before. She sent me to Sunday School and Church on a regular basis. She even had my Easter Suits tailored made and I got a special outfit for Easter Monday for the Easter Egg Hunt.

I missed my siblings and really had mixed emotions about leaving Miss Flossie too. After all, I had started Chestnut Street Primary School in kindergarten and had finished fourth grade in Portsmouth, VA with her. She even paid a lady to bring my raincoat, boots, and umbrella to me at school because it started to rained in the afternoon. She didn't want me to get wet.

My dad really liked for me to live with Miss Flossie. He would come to visit me and he even suggested to Miss Flossie to legally adopt me. I don't think my mom would have agreed with the adoption. After all, I was her baby. I was my Dad's baby too. He even took me to Philadelphia, PA to meet his stepmother and his sisters. That was a very enjoyable trip. They just spoiled me and I hated to leave them. He brought me back to Miss Flossie's house. She spoiled me too! However, I missed my real family very much. I was a well off princess in Portsmouth and a poor little rag doll in Norfolk. I really didn't know who I wanted to be. I'm talking about mixed emotions or whatever. I really wanted to live in both cities.

My parents soon separated. I guess it was due to my dad's drinking problem. When I was only seven years old, my dad expired with sclerosis of the liver. That really upset me and it was quite a while before I finally accepted the realization that he wasn't coming back. Miss Flossie was very understanding while I was experiencing the grieving process.

She even let me sleep with her for a few nights. I didn't have to dust so perfectly for a few days. She was a very loving and caring person.

I didn't seem to miss my folks as much as I did when my dad was living. The most difficult part was when my family would come to visit me on Sundays. My mom would ask me to go and get her a big glass of ice water. Miss Flossie's icebox was located all the way on the back porch. I'd find the biggest glass in the cabinet and I'd chip my little heart out trying to make a very special glass of ice water for my mom. I was hoping she would let me go back home with them. Much to my surprise, when I returned to the front porch, my family would not be there. They had left me again and I would go into the bathroom and just cry and cry! I can't remember what happened to that special glass of water that I had worked so hard to make it for my real mother. I finally went to bed and cried myself to sleep. I never understood why I couldn't go home with my family. I actually thought I was in the "Farm School." That was what we called the reformatory for bad children. I just didn't know what I had done wrong. Oh, let me tell you about an experience when I did something wrong and I did not know immediately that I had done something wrong until after I did it. Let me start at the very beginning. One morning Miss Flossie

told me to go to the store around the corner and buy a box of Octagon Washing Powder and I could buy me a cone of ice cream. Well, I went straight across the street to the drugs store and got me a double dip of strawberry ice cream on a regular cone. Oh, that ice cream was so good and I was still licking on it when I arrived at the corner grocery store which was really two blocks away. I got to the counter and I told the lady that I wanted a box of Octagon Washing Powder. The lady put the washing powder in a bag and asked me for the money. I handed her the nickel and then she told me that was not enough money. She asked me how much did I pay for the ice cream? All of a sudden, I just couldn't remember. The lady told me to go back home and get another nickel. Well, I slowly walked out of the store and then I realized that I was supposed to get only one dip of ice cream for five cents and save the dime for the washing powder. When it hit me that I had made such a horrible mistake, I threw that cone of ice cream down in the gutter and walked slowly back home. The strawberries just didn't seem so sweet anymore. I knew that I was going to get a whipping and as I got closer and closer to 723 County Street, the tears began to flow. When she asked me, where was the washing powder? I told her that I didn't have enough money to pay for it. She saw the dried up ice cream all around my lips and she knew why I didn't have enough money. She got the belt, grabbed me and put my head between her thighs and she beat my behind until it was on fire. I mean that was the worst whipping I had ever had. Why didn't they have child abuse laws back in those days? My hips hurt for days. I really thought I was in the "Farm School." I don't really like strawberry ice cream now. I try to think things through before I make decisions even until this very day. Seems like I can still feel those stings she put on me. After that beating, I really wanted to go home with my real family.

I prayed and asked God to please let me go home and live with my family. The next day, I'd soon get over the disappointment and would return to my happy- go- lucky self. I really loved people and when a bullying child would put a little stick on my shoulder and knock it off, I'd say, "Let's be friends." I'd give the girl a piece of my candy. She'd still beat me up, made me cry, tore the bow off my dress and pulled the ribbons off my hair. Miss Flossie would fuss at me and tell me that if I come home another day like that she was going to wear me out. When I'd see those rough kids, most of the time, I'd take off running, but when they caught me this time I had to fight back. Soon they left me alone. That was real bullying, even in elementary school. You know the bullying must go!

My mom remarried a few years later, and they insisted that I come home to live with my family. All this moving back and forth had to take its toll on me. I was a well-to-do **spoiled brat** when I was with Miss Flossie and a **rebellious preteen** when I was with my family. They didn't seem like family to me anymore. Especially, since my stepfather was in the picture now. I couldn't understand why I could only have one piece of fried chicken when I lived with them, but when I was with Miss Flossie, I could eat the whole chicken.

I was so confused when I was with them. I really thought they were mean, but I still loved them and wanted to live with them most of the time. I knew I was not in the farm school now but I wondered where was I? My mom had a good job at the Naval Air Station, in Norfolk, Virginia at this time.

It was a quite a transition moving from Portsmouth, VA back to Norfolk, VA. My mom's and my stepfather's rules were very different from Miss Flossie's. I was used to having my way most of the time and that was not the case in this new house in the Norview neighborhood. I hated washing the finger prints off the walls and washing the dishes all the time. Ironing was no fun.

I transferred to Oakwood Elementary and enjoyed having my brother, Carl at the same school with me. Other than that, it was quite a challenge to get accustomed to these new rules. I had to do all the ironing, some cooking, most of the cleaning, very little time on the phone, and a lot of time helping take care of my two nieces and my little sister. There was very little time to be a child or just be me. I was so unhappy.

Just getting to know my stepfather was almost unbearable. I really loved my brother, Carl but he could be almost unbearable too. My other two brothers had joined the Army and Air Force. Carl soon left for the Air Force too. I really missed him a lot. My older sister had moved to New Jersey and I didn't have anyone to

have a conversation. Now let's go way back when I was with my family in Liberty Park.

I remembered an incident when Carl told on me and I was very embarrassed. That was the year Miss Flossie let me start the second grade in Norfolk at Liberty Park Elementary School, with my family.

Basically, I was an honest child but this was a case of desperate need, you got to do what you have to do. Carl told my teacher that my mom did not give me that dollar I had just given her for my workbook. I didn't really steal it. I really had found it tied up in a handkerchief on the ground, on my way to school. The teacher kept telling me that I was going to fail the second grade, if I didn't hurry up and pay for my workbook. My mom kept telling me that she just didn't have a dollar because she had to pay bills. I really didn't want to repeat the second grade. The teacher sent the dollar to the office to the student who had reported that she had lost it on the way to school. That teacher saw how I was crying my heart out. Actually, she paid for the workbook for me. I'll never forget Mrs. Darden, my second grade teacher. After my dad passed, I begged my mom to let me go back to Miss Flossie's and I transferred back to Portsmouth that same year. Just three years later and now I'm back with my Norfolk family again.

There were several memorable occasions that I'll never forget while I was at Oakwood with my brother, Carl. One day the principal, Mr. Hughes came into my class and asked the class, "Who could spell the word, inconceivable?" He gave me a quarter because I was the only one who spelled it correctly. That really made my day and I spent it on ice cream and

cake. Another time, the main character in the Christmas play got the chicken pox. I was selected to take her place with only a few weeks to learn all of her speaking, singing, and dancing parts. Everyone said I was great, even my brother, Carl. I made it to the finals in the spelling bee and my mom was crowned the Queen of the PTA because she raised the most funds in the contest. That year was the highlight of my elementary life.

I completed the sixth grade at Oakwood Elementary School and went on to graduate from Ruffner Junior High (RJH). The only thing I can recall about going there was getting up very early to ride the bus to school and getting home late in the evening. I didn't have any time to go outside to play. The books were used, but that wasn't anything new. However, I really did like changing classes, taking physical education, and homemaking. Those adolescent years leaves, a lot to be desired. I was very happy when I graduated from that school. I could hardly wait to go to Booker T. Washington High School (BTW). It was the only high school for African American students in the city of Norfolk, VA. The books and the building were subnormal. That didn't matter, I'd be with my friends, so I thought.

A change is going to come, much to my surprise. It wasn't the kind of change I wanted to happen. How could anything go wrong in a beautiful new-looking school?

Chapter 2

Rough Times at Norview High

Dear Everybody,

Whether you are currently enrolled in a school, all of you have been your mother's student. Remember, who was your first teacher? We've all been home schooled in one way or another and we are never too old to learn. We are constantly learning something each and every day. I could hardly wait for the summer to end so that I could attend (BTW). Well, as soon as I finished Ruffner Jr. High, my sister asked me, if I'd like to come up to New Jersey to keep my nieces while she worked. I told her I'd loved to come to New Jersey and baby sit for her. Believe me that was a fun filled summer and I was in no hurry to come back to Virginia. I was elated with joy when my sister asked me if I'd like to go to school up there because she needed me to stay with the girls before and after school. She had to be to work very early and didn't get home until late. Oh, this was like the icing on the cake. I already missed my friends back home, but I knew I'd make new friends. Just to be away from those ole strict rules and my stepfather made it well worthwhile. We went shopping for school clothes and school supplies. I was just thrilled to be going to any high school and especially one in the north. I couldn't go to sleep on Labor Day night because I knew I'd be going to West Orange High School (WOH) tomorrow.

The school sat high up on a hill and it was a very old brick building. The inside was like a brand new building.

I'd never been in a school like this one. Everybody was so warm and friendly. I actually thought I was dreaming. They had new books and the library had so many books. The cafeteria was very clean and the food was very good too. It seemed like everything about this school was perfect compared to what I was used to seeing. It didn't bother me one bit that I had to go back to Spanish I because I just couldn't keep up in that class with every word had to be spoken and written in Spanish II. I was much more comfortable back in Spanish I. My counselor had been stationed at the Norfolk Naval Base and he checked on me daily. He was the one who changed my schedule so I could perform on my own level in Spanish I. My best friend was Judy Gainer. She and her Mom were very kind and considerate to me. I thought I had died and went to heaven. There was no bullying at this school. I was so happy. Judy and I had lots of fun!

We enjoyed going to the movies together on Saturdays. Her mom would pick me up and we would have fun together. I was shocked when I realized that there were only four African Americans in the whole school. I think most of these kids were quite wealthy based on their clothes and the cars a lot of them drove. I just fell in love with (WOH) and they fell in love with me.

During the winter holidays, I got the sad news that I had to come home because the kitchen stove had exploded and my mom's hands were covered with bandages and she needed my help. I was so sorry that she got injured, but I sure hated to have to leave (WOH). I wondered was I born for bad luck or what. Well, I didn't have any choice so the next thing I knew was enrolling in (BTW). I was so glad to see my friends, but I was very lonely for (WOH). It took me a while to get use to all the negatives that I didn't have to deal with at (WOH). I felt like Cinderella after midnight. The condition of the building was so different and every Monday we had to keep our coats on because the furnace didn't work. The books were used and marked in and some of the pages were missing. Several days the rain leaked through the ceiling and we had to move our desks so that we didn't get wet. I just couldn't believe the differences between the two schools. The teachers were marvelous and I finally got myself together. I'll never forget how we had to get up very early to ride two buses all the way downtown to get to (BTW) and getting home so late that there was no play time. We had to purchase bus tickets in order to ride the school buses. That was an added expense for my parents. When my mom asked me if I'd like to go to Norview High School (NHS), I didn't hesitate to say yes and later asked her the following questions:

1. Will I be able to walk to school?
2. Will I get new books?
3. Will the building be better than (BTW)?
4. Will I be able to sleep later and get home earlier?

My mom answered all of my questions with yes. The first thought that came to my mind was that going to (NHS) will be just like going to (WOH).

I was concerned about leaving my friends again then I remembered all the friends I made at (WOH). My mom emphasized that she believed that I would get a better education and that I have a right to go to the school nearest my home. I didn't have any idea of what the fight for integration would be like. I knew I loved people and I was determined to be an excellent Freedom Fighter. I did not expect any bullying. I was so excited to be going to another mostly all white school. I could hardly wait.

Chapter 3

The Fight for Integration

Dear Freedom Fighters,

Yes, we are all freedom fighters and it started all the way back during the time when we fought for our religious freedom from England. Just think about all the wars we've been involved including the world wars, Vietnam, and in Iraq. We've had a lot of experience fighting for our freedom and especially during our fight for civil rights. I know you recall President Lyndon B. Johnson signing those Civil Rights Acts in the 1960's. Our fight for school desegregation started in 1954 with Brown v. Board of Education. Right now, we are going to focus on how I became a freedom fighter. Perhaps we will review our history following the above case later. The NAACP deserves all the credit for getting me involved. My mom signed the application requesting that I attend the school nearest my home. Several men from the NAACP came to our home one evening and explained the right to attend the school nearest one's home.

The first part of the summer in 1958 was not a lot of fun for me because those 151 African American students who applied to go to the school nearest their homes had to be tested. I really don't remember exactly how many days I was tested but I know they were testing me when I really wanted to be in West Orange, NJ. There were many different kinds of tests like I.Q. tests, academic tests, psychological tests, and interviews with the school board.

Those interviews were very stressful. We went to the school board building to a conference room that had all these Caucasian men firing questions so fast that before I could answer one question another man would yell out another question. It was actually frightening to me. I remember the question that asked "What will you do if someone calls you a n----- and what will you do if someone fights you?" Two questions at one time were a bit much. I answered them the way I had been trained and said "I'll just ignore that nonsense. Believe me that is exactly what I did. I didn't really experience any fights other than being pushed and being called lots of names especially the n--- word, Charley Brown, Coon, and many others that I don't remember right now. I got so tired of taking those tests that I told my mom that I was going to mark all the answers wrong. She threatened me if I did that and I told her it was a joke. I think I really meant it, but I was afraid.

Well, I finally receive a letter indicating that I was one of the 7 who would attend Norview High School. I went back to NJ for the rest of the summer.

When I came home from NJ I didn't want to go anywhere or even talk to Allen. I really was not happy to be home. My mom told me she had promised Allen that I would call him as soon as I got home. He had made her a cake for her while I was gone and had talked to her quite a bit. They had really got to know each other quite well. I told her I'd call him later because I was very tired from that long bus ride from NJ. She reminded me that I had a meeting at the Covenant Church and that I should call him now so that he would drive me to the church. I called him and he was happy to drive me to church. The meeting was a training session about how to deal with reporters, negative phone calls, cross burning and conducting ourselves in a mannerly way no matter what the situation may be. The meeting was very informative and was food for thought. The opening of school was very near and I couldn't wait to go to (NHS). The schools didn't open and the next news that I got was that I would be going to school at The Historic First Baptist Bute Street Church in September 1958.

Oh, I forgot to explain to you why the six schools the 17 of us had applied to attend were closed. Take one guess. You got it.

Now, we are going to discuss Massive Resistance in VA in 1958. On the other hand, you have homework; go on the Internet and learn all about it. I'm not a real historian, so I'll tell more about me. Allen and I dated in August and September. Can you believe we got married on October 14, 1958? Guess what, I was not pregnant either. We were in love!

Remember, Allen Jr. wasn't born until January 14, 1960. Notice all the major events in my life that occurred on 14th. Is it magic or what? You do the math.

Now, I refused to relive those horrible days at, (NHS) but I'll share a few of the hard times (NHS). The first day, February 2, 1959, was not a welcoming day for the Norfolk 17. The National Press waited along the sidewalk leading all the way up to

the doorstep along with armed policemen. We exited the NAACP car that had transported us from our homes to school. All Anglo Saxons were lined up along the sidewalk leading up to the main entrance, policemen, men, women, and national newsmen with microphones and photographers with cameras.

All I can remember saying was, "No comment, no comment." They were pushing those microphones in our faces, constantly. I was really scared.

They were looking very angry throwing rocks, sticks, etc. at us. They called us terrible names and they spit at us. Did the policemen stop them? No, no, we were on our own and I must admit, I was scared to death. I walked very quickly to the door. Once inside the auditorium, I sat down in a front row and all the students in that section got up and moved to the rear. I wanted to move with them, but I realized they were moving away from me. I felt safer up front near the teachers, so I remained in my seat up front. Well, let's move right along. Students' names were called to come up and get their schedules and move on to their homerooms. Guess whose name was not called? Of course, they didn't have one for me. After holding my hand up for a while, I went up to one of the teachers and asked for my schedule. She told me she didn't have it. I asked where do I go to get my schedule? She told me to try the office and I asked her where is the office? She told me to go up stairs and I would see it. I didn't know if I needed to go to the right or left, anyway I finally entered the office. I stood at the counter and waited and waited. Finally, I said I needed to pick up my schedule. The lady took her own good time, and finally put the schedule on the counter. I looked at it and I didn't see physical education. I asked why it wasn't there? She said it was for my safety and she mumbled under her breath that I would cause the showers to get dirty too. I asked which way was my homeroom? She said try one-way and if I didn't find it, just try the other way. I finally found it and as soon as I sat down, the students started moving their desks away from mine. The teacher didn't say a word. She went on having students introduce themselves. I don't remember introducing myself and that was okay. We only had school for a half-day and I was so happy when the bell rang. There was a very well dressed man waiting for me to show me to the main exit. That was the best part of the first day! I never found out who that man was but I felt safe walking with him. That was the longest half day I had ever spent in school. I could hardly wait to get to my first home and later to my second home (my in law's home) in Liberty Park a low rent housing project. It was the area where I lived when I was with my Mom and Dad in Norfolk. What a coincidence? I thought I'd live there eternally. Especially, when Allen and I finally got our first home right in that same neighborhood, good ole Liberty Park. I walked up to the office and applied for that home. Especially, when I learned that we were expecting our first child, I knew we needed our own living space. My in-laws had eleven children, three girls and eight boys. Two of the older ones had moved out, on their own. All the boys slept in two sets of bunk beds in one of the three bedrooms. The girls slept on the pull-out sofa in the living room. We had our bedroom and Allen's parents slept in the other bedroom. That was a full house, believe me! Attending (NH) out-of district was a super duper challenge. I was a school girl in day and a grown woman at night after I left my Mom's home. I went to the lodge house in Oakwood to do my homework as soon as I left (N H). Next, Allen picked me up and then we went home in almost down town Norfolk. Is that going to the school nearest my home? You figure that out or do the math. Remember, reading is my area of expertise!

All the remainder days at (N H) didn't change that much from the first day except for an incident I shall never forget. I had to carry all my books around all day because I was too afraid to go inside the locker room. Just like not using the restroom, it was too dangerous to risk going anywhere adults were not present. Therefore, I could hardly wait to get home from school without having an accident on myself. Now, back to carrying my books all day, a very short boy ran up to me and knocked all my books out of my hands and nobody helped me pick them up. I was so afraid someone might hurt me while I was picking up my books. God was on my side once again, thank you Lord!

I was almost late for my next class. That wasn't the worst part, when I felt something wet on the back of my hand, it was bleeding. I had been cut and I was so relieved that it wasn't anything serious, that I just ignored it. I didn't tell anyone about that frightening experience for a very long time. Oh, another embarrassing incident occurred in American History class. We were studying about the civil war and I was told that I would have been one of the house slaves because the sun had not baked my skin like the other slaves who worked in the fields. I would have had to cook, clean, and take care of the children. The boys started calling me" house slave" and" house n----." No one said any other word. I wanted to change into an ant and just crawl right out of that classroom. I never got used to being called the n--- word, Charlie Brown, Coon etc. This went on all day long, especially between classes and in the cafeteria. When I sat down at a table in the cafeteria or library, all the students would get up and move away.

You know that all that bullying had to go! Guess what, the bullying never went away!

Oh, I almost forgot to tell you about our ride home in the NAACP car on the first day. I thought I'd never get home because we rode around and around. The driver finally told us that a car full of husky-looking white men were following us and he had to lose them before he could let anyone out of the car. It was almost dark before I got home. I really thought I would have an accident on myself, the Lord took good care of me and I made it home after we lost those scary men. Thank God for that! I remained at (N H) for that semester and believe me, I never returned to that school from hell!

Now, I must give credit where credit is due. I can't recall a single girl calling me names. I remember one girl who looked at me as if to say, I want to be your friend, but I'm afraid what might happen to me. She didn't smile or frown at me. Seven years later, I saw that same girl in the emergency room in DePaul Hospital and she had that same friendly look on her face. I wanted to talk to her, but all the negative actions returned and I just let it go. Now, I wish I could find her because she reminded me of my friend at (WHO), Judy Gainer. She really was a true friend. All that bullying really got the best of me. I was so happy to be expecting our first child because I knew that I did not have to return to (N H).

Chapter Four
High School & Universities

Dear Family and Friends,

Allen and I conceived our first child after being married for six months. Everything was not bad while attending (N H). We were so happy to have Allen Jr. and when he was eighteen months old, along came Alvalon. When they were three and one I returned to (BTW) as a full time day student and graduated in June12, 1963. I remained home with my babies for two years until they were old enough to attend Liberty Park Nursery. Reliable baby sitters were hard to find.

One quit on me while we were home for the winter break. I didn't find out that I didn't have a baby sitter until I took them to her on the first day after the break. I nearly had a heart attack. I begged her to keep them that day and I wouldn't bring them back again. She had a new group of children. The Lord found me another baby sitter and I could never thank Him enough. He may not come when you want Him, but He is always on time. I thanked the Lord for that blessing. This time I stayed home with my babies until they were five and three. I started Norfolk State University (NSU) in 1965 and graduated in 1968. My last son was conceived my first month of my teaching career. What a surprise! The IUD just died on me. I was not a happy camper. However, life goes on. It was quite a challenge, but I was determined to become a teacher and I started teaching for Norfolk Public Schools (NPS) in 1968. I retired from (NPS) in 1996. While working for (NPS) I earned a Master of Science Degree in 1975, and a Certificate of Advanced Studies Degree in 1983. The final degree is a Doctorate of Humane Letters in 2008 after I retired from (NPS). All of these degrees were earned at Old Dominion University (ODU). The last one is my favorite! Just think, look what I received after enduring all that bullying that I didn't deserve. Another one of the Norfolk 17, Dr. Patricia Turner received the Doctor of Humane Letters from ODU at the earlier graduation on the same day that I received mine. We were the only two of the 17 that had earned Master Degrees from ODU. We were treated royally throughout that whole weekend! That was a weekend I shall never forget! Old Dominion University is a school that I hold a special place in my heart! Mr. John Broderick, the president is a very unique individual, I'll never forget him!

Norfolk State University (NSU) invited The Norfolk 17 over several times to share our experiences and answer questions. We were treated very kindly with certificates, receptions, and honorariums. The love in the room was always very apparent and over flowing. Dr. Charles Ford, Chairman of the History Department was responsible for The Norfolk 17 receiving a monetary honorarium and a silver framed certificate.

My certificate stated that The History Department at Norfolk State University honors Delores Johnson Brown for her courageous effort as a member of the Norfolk 17. There is no place like home!

There's a saying that says, "You can always go home when you can't go anywhere else."

Invite me, I'll be there!

Chapter Five
Resolutions, Awards & Certificates

We have been honored by the COMMONWEALTH OF VIRGINIA General Assembly with the HOUSE JOINT RESOLUTION NO. 552.

It was agreed to by the House of Delegates on March 5, 2008 and the Senate on March 6, 2008. It opened with following statement:

"Commending the Norfolk 17 on the occasion of the 50th anniversary of their struggle to integrate the public schools of Norfolk."

The city of Norfolk honored us for our bravery with the RESOLUTION NO.1141: "A Resolution Recognizing the Historic Role of The Norfolk 17 in Bringing Virginia's Massive Resistance Movement to an End." The City Council really rolled out the red carpet for a whole week of activities in celebration of our 50th anniversary of integrating the public schools in Norfolk, VA. The date of this resolution is February 26, 2002. Our 1959 group photo is hanging up in the halls of The Norfolk City Hall. Our current photos are hanging up in the halls of Norview High School. There is a monument outside the new (NHS) that list our names.

Norfolk Public Schools, presented us with the Resolution of the Norfolk City School Board which ended with the following:

"Now Therefore Be It Resolved that the Norfolk City School Board honors with sincere appreciation the strength, dedication, sacrifice, and resolve of the Norfolk 17, their families, and many others for their tireless efforts to ensure that quality public –education is a viable and attainable resource for all." We were also given zippered leather notebooks with the NPS logo on them.

The Norfolk Public Library Foundation included the Norfolk 17 in their 2009 Norfolk Historical Calendar on the February pages. The caption under our 1959 photo read: "These 17 people pioneered the desegregation of Norfolk Public Schools on 2 February, 1959—50 years ago this month. They stand in front of First Baptist Church, Bute Street, where they tutored during the fall of 1958, when the formally all-white Norfolk junior and senior high schools to which they had been assigned remained closed."

The Certificate of Educational Advancement was presented to the Norfolk 17 on being inducted into the New Journal and Guide's Hall of Fame on August 8, 2004. We were also inducted into the Hampton Roads African American Sports Hall of Fame Eight – Annual Induction Ceremony on October 30, 2004 with the Special Recognition Award. It stated: "The Norfolk 17 for 'Leading the Way' For Your Service to Fight for Freedom, Equality, Justice and the Rights of All People to Dream and Aspire to Those Dreams." It was signed by the Chairman and the President of the AASHF.

The Historic First Baptist Bute Street Church in Norfolk, Virginia presented a Certificate of Recognition to Delores Johnson Brown on January 4, 1998. The following quotation from Dr. Martin Luther King Jr. was at the bottom of the certificate: "The ultimate measure of a man is not where he stands in moments of comfort and convenience, but where he stands at times of challenge and controversy." It was signed by the pastor, Dr. Robert G. Murray and the Cultural Committee Chairperson, Rosalind B. Jennings. The title of the program was, "Remembering The Role of First Baptist Church In The Civil Rights Movement." A reception followed the program.

We have also been honored again on Freedom Sunday on July 6, 2008 at the Historic First Baptist Bute Street Church, who opened their doors to us when we were locked out of the Norfolk Public Schools. I was presented another Certificate of Recognition from the Board of Christian Education from Mt. Olive Baptist Church in Norfolk, Virginia on January 21, 2007. It stated, "Presented to Delores Johnson, a member of the Norfolk17, whose unwavering sacrifices of yesterday made it possible for the children of today to be educated with equality, dignity, and unity." It was signed by the Director, Board of

Christian Education and Deacon Joseph P. Edney Jr, Chairman, Board of Deacons. Many churches, schools, organizations, and the U.S. Navy have invited me and other members of the Norfolk 17 to speak and they have expressed their gratitude in many ways.

Dr. Patricia Turner, another one of the Norfolk 17 and I got to meet Carl Brashear, the first Black Naval Diver. We thanked him for being such a hero. He told us that we were the real heroes. Dr. Turner was one of the guest speakers at the NAVAIRES Norfolk's Bl ack History Month Program 2004. We both were presented with Certificates of Appreciation, signed by Captain E.D. Watson, U.S. Naval Reserve, given this 27th day of February 2004. It stated: "Presented in appreciation of your contribution of time and personal effort. The challenges you faced in the times of school integration make an intriguing and fascinating story; one that be forgotten by any who hear it. Your personal example of integrity is commendable. Thanks again for your participation in the program." That was a day I'll never forget either!

Chapter Six

Meet all Of The Norfolk 17

Although it was quite a challenge, if I had to do it all over again, I would do it without any hesitation. Thanks to everyone who has been kind to me as a result of being one of the Norfolk 17, especially my Norfolk 17 family:

Delores Johnson Brown
LaVera Forbes Brown
Louis Cousins
Frederick Alvarez Gonsouland
Andrew Heidelberg
Geraldine Talley Hobby
Edward Jordan
Olivia Driver Lindsay
Lolita Portis
Betty Jean Reed
*Johnnie Rouse
*James Turner
Patricia Turner
Carol Wellington
*Claudia Wellington
Patricia Godbolt White
*Reginald Young
*Deceased

Chapter Seven

Closing, From the Heart

Family, Friends, Other Readers, too
Lend me your ears for closing these years, only a few.
I humbly confess, I really tried my best,
To tell my life story, with
God and all His glory,
Through my trials and tribulations,
He taught me to pray, all the way in adoration.
Thank you, Thank you, and Thank you!

Chapter Eight

Happy Birthday to Me

Yes, I must close this autobiography with the time of my life, my seventieth birthday party held at the Greenbrier Country Club in Chesapeake, Virginia. Two hundred and fifty family and friends were invited and a few extras attended. That's okay we had fun!

The early arrivals were serenaded by Eric Taylor, our violinist for the evening. Hors d'oeuvres were served while my Bridge Club, The Chesapeake Holidays, Inc. checked in guest and ushered them to their assigned seats. The ballroom was so beautifully decorated in my sorority's colors, red and white. Nancy Hawkins did an outstanding job with the white feathers and red roses on the tables in tall vases. White chair covers with red and white tablecloths and napkins on the tables made me feel like a Delta Queen. Allen escorted me into the ballroom and we entered as Melvin White, our deejay played "Here comes the Bride." That was a joke, since we couldn't afford a wedding when we got married. We were "po" more than pore.

We were happily in love! I put the scarf over my head that was a part of my white gown. Eve Moore, the mistress of ceremony and Allen's aunt did an outstanding job of following the program as printed. She gave the Welcome and Dr. Rose Ward, the former mayor's wife, gave the Birthday Prayer.

"The Occasion" was presented by Eve Moore in a very unique manner using a quiz entitled, How well do you know Delores? That was so much fun, everyone claimed to have won. Rev. Angela Taylor gave the "Blessing." Dinner was served and prior to serving the birthday cake, Stevie Wonder's Birthday Song was sung and a toast was given with champagne or apple cider. The birthday cake was served next. Pat Painter and the Seniors in Motion really put on a super rendition of line dancing. The violinist and the deejay continued to entertain us. Tributes were given by representatives of the following:

Holiday Bridge Dr. Carmelita Williams
D.S.T. Sorority Stephanie Gordon
Drifters Dr. Rowena Wilson
The Links Inc. Mary Redd Nelson
Maude Armstrong # 190 Sylvia Downey Moles
Saundra Eaddy &Dr. Sheila Russ
Norfolk 17 Dr. Patricia Turner
Assoc. U. Women Dr. Elenor Jones
ABA & DBC Betty Warren
The Family Allen Jr. & Allen Sr.
The Honoree Dr. Delores J. Brown
Closing Prayer Eld. Shirley Ross,
Allen's aunt
Line and Couple Dancing
Acknowledgments
Many thanks for your generosity, love, and support!
Love,
Delores

Hostesses
Holiday Bridge, Inc. ChesapeakeChapter
Mrs. Perdethia Lowery, Chair
Mrs. Gloria Brown
Mrs. Wanza Dodson
Dr. Bertha Escoffery
Mrs. Maxine Green
Dr. Sarah Lang
Mrs. Jo Ann Pugh
Dr. Carmelita Williams
Mrs. Vivian West, Honorary

Mrs. Evelyn Williams, Honorary
Mrs. Carol Hillery, Guest
(Baltimore Chapter)

Customized Candy Bar Wrappers
Ms. Patricia Ross

Decorations

Mrs. Nancy Hawkins
Mrs. Cecelia Pretlow
Mrs. Brenda Melniczak
Mr. James Melniczak

Photographer & Videographer
Mr. Reggie and Mrs. Deborah Burkett

Programs & Invitations
By
Ms. Junell L. Banks
THE PHOTO GALLERY

NEWS ARTICLES

Rundate:
05/17/1994

NORFOLK'S HISTORIC SCHOOL FIGHT\ FORTY YEARS AGO, THE LAND'S HIGHEST COURT SENT A MESSAGE TO AMERICA: SEGREGATED SCHOOLS VIOLATE THE RIGHTS OF INDIVIDUALS GUARANTEED BY THE 14TH AMENDMENT TO THE CONSTITUTION. THOUGH THE RULING SEEMED TO END THE DEBATE, THE BATTLE WAS JUST BEGINNING. IT REACHED A FEVER PITCH IN NORFOLK IN 1959.

BY LISE OLSEN, STAFF WRITER

Color photos\ LAWRENCE JACKSON/Staff\ \ \ PAUL AIKEN/ Staff\ Delores Brown, center, at Norview High School in 1959.\ \ \ Graphics\ Photos\ MASON ANDREWS: As a young gynecologist in 1958, Andrews met with other Norfolkians behind closed doors about how the schools could be peacefully reopened and integrated. "We'd have meetings and we'd pull the shades down, so no one could see who was talking about such seditious things.'

Andrews Andrews and others foresaw potential economic disaster for the city if the schools stayed closed. So they went to friends and co-workers and asked them to join forces against the powerful City Council and mayor. "It was just something that didn't seem to be right. It was a matter of how to fix it.'

Today, Andrews is the mayor.

Bernard Jarvis: A member of the Crestwood High School Class of 1970, Jarvis fought hard as a student to keep the popular black high school school in Chesapeake from closing as part of the district's desegregation plan. But Jarvis, parents and the NAACP all lost the fight. The school closed after graduation in 1971. The other schools that Jarvis attended also have been razed or converted for other uses.

"As an adult, I look back on my early elementary and secondary ... education with some sadness. In one respect, I think it prepared me to handle just about any kind of academic or life experience that one could have,' said Jarvis, assistant vice president for finance at Howard University in Washington D.C. "But none of those institutions that served me so well have survived intact to this day. Which to me is disheartening.'

Henry L. Marsh III: Marsh, a member of the Virginia General Assembly, was just a kid in the 1950s when his aunt, Amy Palmer, Marsh fought to integrate the schools in Isle of Wight County. But he grew up to be one of the main lawyers in the NAACP's legal fight to desegregate schools through busing in the 1960s and 1970s. Marsh handled about 40 cases across Virginia, including most of the ones in Hampton Roads.

Today he looks back with satisfaction at the changes that resulted from his work. "I think it's clear that in every case we have ended the formal segregation of schools on the basis of race, and had segregation not been ended it would have resulted in a continuation of conditions that led to the Brown decision in the first place.'

E.E. Brickell: In 1959, Brickell was principal of an alternative night school run by segregationists in South Norfolk. He continued to deal with desegregation and busing as superintendent in three local districts: Franklin, South Norfolk (now Chesapeake), and Virginia Beach. In Franklin, he drew up a plan that kept schools desegregated well into the 1970s.

Gerrymandering, delaying tactics, and when all else failed, diplomacy were the tools he used as a Southern superintendent forced to desegregate and then bus students for integration. When busing came to Virginia Beach, he sought - and got - help from the black community to make it peaceful.

"A lot of good people helped make it work.'

\ \ TIMELINE

March 1954: Rear Adm. T.B. Brittain, Norfolk Naval Base commanding officer, requests that the Norfolk School Board integrate Benmoreell, an elementary school on federal property operated by the board. The Navy already had integrated its other facilities. But the board refuses and later closes the school.

May 1954: The U.S. Supreme Court, in its landmark Brown vs. Board decision, rules that school segregation violates the guarantees of equal protection afforded by the 14th Amendment.

September 1955: Norfolk Catholic High admits 12 blacks to its freshman class under the directive of the bishop of the Diocese of Richmond. It is the area's first integration.

May 1956: A lawsuit is filed by the NAACP to end segregation in Norfolk - the first such suit in South Hampton Roads.

September 1956: Massive Resistance laws are approved by the Virginia General Assembly to cut off state funds to any school that integrates.

August 1958: Under court pressure, Norfolk School Board admits 17 blacks to six senior and junior highs.

September 1958: Gov. J. Lindsay Almond Jr. takes over six Norfolk schools and closes them to stop the 17 African-American students from entering. That locks out 10,000 children from schools. About 4,500 enroll in private tutoring programs; many eventually leave the city or drop out.

January 1959: State Supreme Court strikes down Massive Resistance; U.S. District Court forbids the Norfolk City Council from a related proposal to cut off school funding. A hundred community leaders ask publicly, in a full-page advertisement, for the reopening of schools to avoid economic disaster.

February 1959: All Norfolk schools reopen. 17 blacks attend integrated schools.

September 1962: 37 black students enter Princess Anne County schools; Portsmouth desegregates with 14 black students.

September 1963: Chesapeake (formed by the merger of Norfolk County and South Norfolk) desegregates, with six blacks attending two previously all-white schools in the old county section.

1970s: The pressure to bus students for integration increases. Eventually, all local school districts are forced to adopt more aggressive desegregation plans, either by the courts or by the federal government. By 1974 - 20 years after Brown vs. Board - a majority of black students in most cities attend integrated schools, according to statistics reported by school officials then.

\ \ Photo\ LAWRENCE JACKSON/Staff\ Students and teachers from Bowling Park Elementary School in Norfolk marched through nearby neighborhoods on May 6 to encourage residents to get involved with the city's public schools.\

Color photos\ LAWRENCE JACKSON/Staff\ \ \ PAUL AIKEN/ Staff\ Delores Brown, center, at Norview High School in 1959.\ \ \ Graphics\ Photos\ MASON ANDREWS: As a young gynecologist in 1958, Andrews met with other Norfolkians behind closed doors about how the schools could be peacefully reopened and integrated. "We'd have meetings and we'd pull the shades down, so no one could see who was talking about such seditious things.'

Andrews Andrews and others foresaw potential economic disaster for the city if the schools stayed closed. So they went to friends and co-workers and asked them to join forces against the powerful City Council and mayor. "It was just something that didn't seem to be right. It was a matter of how to fix it.'

Today, Andrews is the mayor.

Bernard Jarvis: A member of the Crestwood High School Class of 1970, Jarvis fought hard as a student to keep the popular black high school school in Chesapeake from closing as part of the district's desegregation plan. But Jarvis, parents and the NAACP all lost the fight. The school closed after graduation in 1971. The other schools that Jarvis attended also have been razed or converted for other uses.

"As an adult, I look back on my early elementary and secondary ... education with some sadness. In one respect, I think it prepared me to handle just about any kind of academic or life experience that one could have,' said Jarvis, assistant vice president for finance at Howard University in Washington D.C. "But none of those institutions that served me so well have survived intact to this day. Which to me is disheartening.'

Henry L. Marsh III: Marsh, a member of the Virginia General Assembly, was just a kid in the 1950s when his aunt, Amy Palmer, Marsh fought to integrate the schools in Isle of Wight County. But he grew up to be one of the main lawyers in the NAACP's legal fight to desegregate schools through busing in the 1960s and 1970s. Marsh handled about 40 cases across Virginia, including most of the ones in Hampton Roads.

Today he looks back with satisfaction at the changes that resulted from his work. "I think it's clear that in every case we have ended the formal segregation of schools on the basis of race, and had segregation not been ended it would have resulted in a continuation of conditions that led to the Brown decision in the first place.'

E.E. Brickell: In 1959, Brickell was principal of an alternative night school run by segregationists in South Norfolk. He continued to deal with desegregation and busing as superintendent in three local districts: Franklin, South Norfolk (now Chesapeake), and Virginia Beach. In Franklin, he drew up a plan that kept schools desegregated well into the 1970s.

Gerrymandering, delaying tactics, and when all else failed, diplomacy were the tools he used as a Southern superintendent forced to desegregate and then bus students for integration. When busing came to Virginia Beach, he sought - and got - help from the black community to make it peaceful.

"A lot of good people helped make it work.'

\\ TIMELINE

March 1954: Rear Adm. T.B. Brittain, Norfolk Naval Base commanding officer, requests that the Norfolk School Board integrate Benmoreell, an elementary school on federal property operated by the board. The Navy already had integrated its other facilities. But the board refuses and later closes the school.

May 1954: The U.S. Supreme Court, in its landmark Brown vs. Board decision, rules that school segregation violates the guarantees of equal protection afforded by the 14th Amendment.

September 1955: Norfolk Catholic High admits 12 blacks to its freshman class under the directive of the bishop of the Diocese of Richmond. It is the area's first integration.

May 1956: A lawsuit is filed by the NAACP to end segregation in Norfolk - the first such suit in South Hampton Roads.

September 1956: Massive Resistance laws are approved by the Virginia General Assembly to cut off state funds to any school that integrates.

August 1958: Under court pressure, Norfolk School Board admits 17 blacks to six senior and junior highs.

September 1958: Gov. J. Lindsay Almond Jr. takes over six Norfolk schools and closes them to stop the 17 African-American students from entering. That locks out 10,000 children from schools. About 4,500 enroll in private tutoring programs; many eventually leave the city or drop out.

January 1959: State Supreme Court strikes down Massive Resistance; U.S. District Court forbids the Norfolk City Council from a related proposal to cut off school funding. A hundred community leaders ask publicly, in a full-page advertisement, for the reopening of schools to avoid economic disaster.

February 1959: All Norfolk schools reopen. 17 blacks attend integrated schools.

September 1962: 37 black students enter Princess Anne County schools; Portsmouth desegregates with 14 black students.

September 1963: Chesapeake (formed by the merger of Norfolk County and South Norfolk) desegregates, with six blacks attending two previously all-white schools in the old county section.

1970s: The pressure to bus students for integration increases. Eventually, all local school districts are forced to adopt more aggressive desegregation plans, either by the courts or by the federal government. By 1974 - 20 years after Brown vs. Board - a majority of black students in most cities attend integrated schools, according to statistics reported by school officials then.

\ \ Photo\ LAWRENCE JACKSON/Staff\ Students and teachers from Bowling Park Elementary School in Norfolk marched through nearby neighborhoods on May 6 to encourage residents to get involved with the city's public schools.\

The U.S. Supreme Court outlawed school desegregation on May 17, 1954, but it took four years for that social revolution to reach Jim Crow Hampton Roads.

Then it swept into Norfolk like a northeaster, pushing the city to the edge of a moral and economic abyss. In September 1958, Gov. J. Lindsay Almond closed Norfolk's white schools under Virginia's policy of Massive Resistance. To keep 17 blacks from getting in, Almond locked out 10,000 whites, closing most of the state's largest school system.

Delores Brown, 16, and other pioneering black teens had to retreat to a church basement for tutoring. Thousands of white students, like 17-year-old Frank Sellew, were forced to shop for schools outside the city.

The nation watched Norfolk, center stage in Virginia's struggle to stonewall integration. It was one of the biggest showdowns between the Southern states and the federal courts.

The locked-out students became known as the "Lost Class of 1959,' after a network TV special that documented how the group dropped out and dispersed.

Worried about the future of those children and the city itself, a group of young fathers and professionals began holding secret meetings. They discussed, remembers Mayor Mason Andrews, the unthinkable: The integrated U.S. Navy would abandon Norfolk. The Navy already had pressured the School Board to integrate an elementary school on the base - the board shut down the school instead.

The stakes were so high that the young men decided to risk financial and social ruin by actively recruiting others to defy the segregationist stand of city and state leaders.

As the months passed, Brown and 16 other teens were carefully coached for the day they would cross the color lines. Their regular lessons included advice on how to handle racial slurs and violence. They were considered heroes to those fighting for integration.

But some thought of them as enemies. One day, Brown got an anonymous call at home encouraging her to drop her application to Norview High School. She didn't consider it. "I was determined that was where I was going to go.'

When Granby High School closed, Sellew briefly thought about dropping out. Instead, he ended up at a night school run by segregationists in South Norfolk, now part of Chesapeake.

For a while, it seemed like an extension of summer vacation: Sellew continued staying out late, going to drive-ins and racing hot rods with his friends. But when Granby remained closed, Sellew and his friends organized a brief protest. They found it ridiculous that 2,000 of them would be locked out because one black teen had applied.

Brown and Sellew's temporary schooling proved to be short-lived. The showdown over admitting the first 17 African-American students came quickly in Norfolk.

By December 1958, two NAACP lawsuits challenging the school closings were making their way through the courts - and into the golf-course conversation of a pair of eminent judges.

Dr. Delores Johnson Brown

Judge Walter E. "Beef" Hoffman, of the U.S. District Court was preparing to release a red-hot decision declaring the school closing illegal when he ran into John W. Eggleston, chief justice of the Virginia Supreme Court, on the greens of the Princess Anne Country Club. Eggleston hinted at a surprise: Virginia's high court also would rule against Massive Resistance, but not before January.

Hoffman, a New Jersey native, decided to wait for the Virginians. "Everyone hated the federal court, but they had some respect for the state Supreme Court,' recalls Hoffman, a senior U.S. District Court judge who heard most of the region's school desegregation and busing cases.

The two decisions, issued on Jan. 19, 1959 - Robert E. Lee's birthday - dealt a double blow to Massive Resistance.

About the same time, a full-page ad ran in the newspaper asking for the schools to be reopened. It was signed by 100 prominent civic and business leaders finally convinced to go public by the quiet protest group.

When the schools reopened on Feb. 2, 1959, the national press waited at the doorstep of Norview High School.

Delores Brown remembers the shouts of reporters and the flashes of cameras as she and two other students arrived at Norview that February day. She was frightened: Protesters had burned a cross in the yard of a black classmate.

Norfolk had posted plainclothes policemen inside the schools. And a Norfolk-based assistant U.S. attorney had hooked up a hot line to the White House for reporting updates on the violence, according to Judge Hoffman.

There was nothing to tell - no violence, no rioting. Norfolk was no Little Rock, where school desegregation had spawned violent scenes recorded by television and imprinted on the national memory.

The national press left after a week. But Brown spent the rest of a lonely year at Norview. She remembers sitting in a drab gray lunchroom at a table all by herself.

"Once I sat down everyone moved. That was really damaging to one's self-esteem.' She would gulp down her food and leave as quickly as possible.

She was barred from physical education. But she was glad, because she feared other students would hurt her during games, or in the unsupervised showers. "I just kept hoping and praying every day that nothing would happen to me.'

No one ever tried to harm her, but someone threw a knife at her friend one day.

Frank Sellew returned to Granby to finish his senior year, though many of his classmates did not. "It kind of broke up the class in a lot of ways,' he said. Some students had moved away or dropped out. Others didn't return because one black student had enrolled.

"It was just a disruption of my life. I wasn't able to foresee how my life would change as a result of integration and working in the school system,' Sellew said.

Norfolk schools had integrated, but that was hardly the end of the fight.

Both Brown and Sellew continued to deal with race relations and integration issues over the next three decades as employees of the Norfolk public schools.

Across Hampton Roads, segregationists continued to try to keep African-American students out of white schools with a variety of tactics: intimidation, gerrymandering of school zones, refusing to transport black students to white schools, court battles, and just plain ignoring the law.

Edward E. Brickell, president of the Medical College of Hampton Roads, used many of those tricks as a former superintendent of schools in three local districts. He said he once turned a creek upside down on a map to avoid integrating school zones.

"I was a segregationist. I know it sounds stupid to black people, but it was nothing personal, it was just the way we were raised.'

But when Brickell was finally forced to comply, black community leaders helped make integration peaceful in Virginia Beach.

The late Norfolk Mayor Fred Duckworth went to the greatest extremes to block desegregation: He used redevelopment powers to demolish hundreds of homes in integrated neighborhoods, where it would have been hard to keep blacks out of neighborhood elementary schools, according to a book by Forrest R. "Hap' White called "Pride and Prejudice: School Desegregation and Urban Renewal in Norfolk, 1950-1959.'

Despite the resistance, most local school districts admitted blacks to white schools in the 1960s, though it was limited to those who specially requested it or lived in white neighborhoods.

By the late 1960s, local schools began to desegregate teaching staffs. Both Sellew and Brown were pioneers in that wave of integration in Norfolk public schools. Sellew went on to integrate the staff of an all-black middle school; Brown integrated the staff of an all-white elementary school.

But most African-American students in the region did not attend integrated schools until the early 1970s, when local school districts were forced to bus students to achieve racial balance, under pressure from the courts and the federal government. That's when traditionally black schools were finally integrated - or closed.

Over the years, Portsmouth and Norfolk school districts lost thousands of students to white flight, though housing shortages, crime and other urban problems contributed to that migration. Those two districts went from majority white to majority black student bodies.

That was perhaps the toughest era for Sellew, who oversaw busing programs first as an assistant principal and then a principal.

"There's a lot of people who did abandon the school district,' he said. "The truth is, sometimes I felt abandoned because I was right in the middle of it. I guess we've fared as well as we have because of the people that have stuck with it.'

Norfolk ended elementary school busing for integration in 1986, partly to attract white students back. The success of that effort has been disputed by Harvard University scholars, but Portsmouth officials plan to imitate it in 1995.

For several years, Delores Brown found herself teaching at an all-black school, Bowling Park, which was resegregated when busing ended. But it didn't really bother her, she said. Now she teaches at Sherwood Forest Elementary, where her second-grade class of white and black students doesn't seem to notice their racial differences.

Forty years after Brown vs. Board of Education, school integration is considered relatively successful in Hampton Roads because there was no violence and because most black students attend integrated schools today. Cities here lost fewer white students by percentage than other urban areas, like Richmond or Petersburg. Virginia Beach and other suburban areas have gradually gained more black students, becoming more integrated now than in the 1950s.

For Frank Sellew, deputy superintendent of Norfolk public schools, the changing dynamics of integration have marked all of his professional life. Now, when he looks back at 1959, he wishes he would have talked to that lonely black student who joined his class at Granby High.

"I feel proud of the fact that it didn't get ugly in Norfolk. I feel more bad ... that we didn't make it easier than we did.'

For Delores Brown, the years have brought an increasing sense of satisfaction for the sacrifices she made as a teenager so many years ago.

"It was well worth it. Now that I have children and grandchildren and I can tell them: 'I did it all for you."

July 7, 2008 story

By Denise Watson Batts

The Virginian-Pilot

NORFOLK

Morning worship at First Baptist Church Norfolk on Bute Street was as much of a homecoming as it was "Freedom Sunday."

John Charles Thomas, former Virginia Supreme Court justice and one of the church's native sons, returned as guest speaker to honor the Norfolk 17, the first African-American students to desegregate Norfolk Public Schools almost 50 years ago.

Their milestone did not come easily, Thomas said, as his voice thundered like a preacher's. In September 1958, six city schools closed under state laws that forbade blacks and whites from attending classes together. The 17 then found a home at First Baptist when the church set up classes to teach courses such as Spanish and English, and how not to fight back when punched and spat on, the most enduring lesson they would need when schools opened in February 1959 and they entered previously all-white schools.

"While the state was practicing Massive Resistance," Thomas said, referring to the laws established to keep schools segregated, "these young people were learning passive resistance. ... We knew that you were soldiers in the army, and we're so glad that First Baptist helped you put on that armor of God."

Freedom Sunday not only honored the 17, but it began a month long celebration of the church's 208th anniversary. First Baptist organized as an integrated church for whites, free blacks and slaves.

More than 1,500 packed its pews for the church service. Ten of the Norfolk 17, along with relatives of those absent or who have died, filled the first three. They swayed with the church's choirs, which laced the service with hymns and civil rights songs, such as "Hold On."

Thomas began his speech with thanks to the 17. He said he was able to attend Maury High in the mid-1960s because of them. But even by his time, Maury was still isolating. Thomas recalled showing a poem he'd written to a teacher; she refused it and told him that she didn't believe a black child could write such a piece.

Though the nation has made progress, Thomas related the struggle for equal rights to science.

"How does physics get into a sermon?" he asked. "Trying not cutting your grass, and see what happens. Try not painting your house, and see what happens," he said, his voice rising.

"Try not fighting for freedom, and see what happens. … It takes energy today. It takes energy tomorrow."

After the service, the honorees hugged old friends and teachers and young people who wanted autographs.

Geraldine Talley Hobby, who entered Northside Junior High School in 1959, now works with programs in New York and Maryland to help families with home ownership, and to help children through mentoring. She began the nonprofits based on the activism she learned from her parents, who pushed her to be on the front lines 50 years ago.

"It's rewarding when you look back and reflect on the path that we led," Hobby said. "I want the youth to recognize that education is important. So many don't realize its importance."

About the Author

Meet Dr. DELORES JOHNSON BROWN, she is a wife, mother, and a twenty-eight year retired educator. She has taught elementary, middle school, and as an adjunct professor at Norfolk State University, her undergraduate alma mater. She earned three graduate degrees at Old Dominion University. She has attended William and Mary University and the University of Virginia. She is retired after a successful and fruitful career in education with the Norfolk Public Schools as a Communication Skills Specialist. An active community volunteer and civic organizer, she is a dedicated member of several organizations, most of them she is the chaplain, including The Links, Moles, Chums, Norfolk Alumnae Chapter of Deltas, Drifters, president of the Holidays Bridge Inc., and Eastern Stars Prince Hall Affiliation. She holds membership at Saint Paul's United Methodist Church as a Lay Leader, and is a recipient of numerous awards. She has been featured in several documentaries; Edward R. Murrow, 1958, WAVY TV, WHRO TV, NORVIEW H.S. 2008-2009, Ed Show MSNBC And, LOCKED OUT, The Fall of Massive Resistance. It was developed at the University of Virginia Center for Politics, WCVE & WHTJ. She has been featured on the cover of two magazines: Crisis Summer 2009, VOL 116/3 and Old Dominion U. Graduate Studies. Her hobbies are traveling, reading, crossword puzzles, bridge, and bowling. She has traveled to most of the states in the U.S.A., and some foreign countries such as Africa, Canada, England, Japan, and Paris. The most recent and enjoyable event of her life was her last birthday celebration held at the Greenbrier Country Club in Chesapeake, VA where she resides with her husband, Allen Brown Sr. Dr. Brown' life is filled with excitement and bullying.

Printed in the United States
By Bookmasters